A LITTLE PUPPY

CHILDREN'S KNOWLEDGE BOOK

WILLIAM SINGLETON

Made with ♥ on the Notion Press Platform
www.notionpress.com

Contents

1. My new family

A short while later, I was able to see,
A nice lady came and asked about me,
"As soon as he can eat on his own,
You will be able to take him home."
I hope it will be soon.
At my house, there is plenty of room.
"He is ready to go now."
She said, "Oh wow.
He can eat,
Here, give him this treat."
It was so yummy.
Felt so good in my tummy.
"Here, let me give you some more."

When you get a chance to go to the store,
She was so sweet;
Then she picked me up off my feet,
Then, she carried me to her car,
It seemed like we went really far;
She left me in the front seat,
To see, I have to be on just two feet.
Sometimes, she goes real fast,
Riding in the car is such a blast.
This is such a thrill,
Can't sit still,
So much fun,
Going fast and don't even run.

2. VET

She called the doctor on her phone,
Said we have to see him before we go home,
Don't know why I have to go to the vet,
I'm not even sick yet;
We got there real soon,
There were a lot of pets there, and there wasn't much room,
One puppy there was just a mutt,
Looked like he needed a fur cut.
A mother dog didn't have a tail to wiggle,
I couldn't help it and started to giggle.
One dog was sick and old,
Kept shivering like he was cold.
Two little puppies didn't look like the others,
I think they were brothers.
A lady was crying because her cat was very sick
Saying, "Please, can the doctor come quick?"
Later, I found out she would be ok.

But will have to stay,
The nurse put us in our own room,
Then said, "The doctor will see you soon."
He gave me a shot,
Now I have a sore spot,
Now I feel sore,
Hope I don't come back there anymore.
It tickled my nose, making me sneeze,
I wanted to say stop that, please.
Then, he was finally done.
Going there wasn't fun.

3. BOY

I love it when the boy comes over;
He laughs when I roll over,
He comes over once in a while,
I will be wagging my tail and smile.
We have so much fun,
He throws a stick, then I chase it and run,
He loves to play with me,
I love it when he stays all day,
He is a nice boy.
Sometimes, we don't even use a toy,
We play with rage,
I need to be careful so I don't gag,
It is called tug of war,
Being little, just slide across the floor,
Hope he comes more often.

4. WALK

Sometimes, she takes me for a walk,
She loves walking with her friend; they like to talk a lot,
She lives down the street to the end,
She puts me on a leash, worried about me going
in the street;
I mostly worry about her big feet,
One time, she stepped on my paw,
Then carried me and kept saying 'awww'.
Just a little sore,
In a little while, it didn't hurt us anymore,
Sometimes, we walk real far,
Then, I won't know where we are,
We will stop at the store, get a drink, and then walk some more.
Sometimes, when it is hotter
I will drink a lot of water;
One time, we stopped under a shade tree
to rest,
I was watching two birds build a nest.

5. PARK

Then we went to the park,
Hope we leave before it gets too dark.
She said I can get out of the car and play,
It looks like it can get spooky at night
when there isn't much light.
I will be chasing the squirrels, but they run too fast,
Still, I had fun, such a blast,
They run up the trees,
Stop and look at me and tease,
No way it can climb trees.
They are too tall
And be afraid to get hurt and fall.
One boy wanted to play, but he wasn't much fun,
Kept squirting me with a squirt gun,
Almost like the time I chewed the garden house,
And water squirted up my nose;
This other boy was so cool that he let me lick his ice cream,
Until his momma saw it, and then she started to scream,
Then the smell on the grill, oh, oh, what a thrill;
When I see food drop
I get up and jump.

6. PARK 2

I went swimming; wow, I can float,
The others are fishing in the boat,
They climb there and fish,
Looks like they are just wishing.
The kids are playing basketball,
For that, I am way too small,
The kites are way high
Up far in the sky.

7. EAT

Big dogs must eat a lot,
Sometimes, I can't eat all I got
O' and when she gives me a rib bone,
She makes me feel so much at home
Before she gives it to me, I can tell,
I can feel just by the smell
Can't believe this big bone is all mine,
Wish I could get these all the time.

8. CHEW

"What do you think what you are doing?
That is my shoes, the way you are chewing,
That is why I bought you chewing toys at the store.
Don't do that anymore,
That is mine,
You won't get a treat next time,
Those are for my feet
No more chewing or no more treats,
The closet is no
That is nowhere you go
You can't go in the closet anymore,"
Now, she closes the door.

9. BATH

Times she will give me a bath
I look silly and start to laugh.
She says she needs

www.ingramcontent.com/pod-product-compliance
Lightning Source LLC
LaVergne TN
LVHW090140160826
845673LV00017B/2811